This book belongs to:

..............................................

## Using This Book

- Encourage your child to find the picture stickers and answer the questions in the book.

- Use the gold star stickers to praise their successes, and to encourage brushing and good dental habits.

- Fill in the 'I will' tasks on the wipe-clean reward chart, and the star targets and rewards. Involve your child in this process, as they will love the sense of responsibility, and the excitement of working towards the treats they've chosen.

- Rewards need not be big, but they should be meaningful to your child: an extra bedtime story, going to the park, or having a friend to play, – something that they enjoy, and that you feel is appropriate to what they have achieved.

- Always keep a positive attitude and remember to focus on their achievements. Never take away stickers or deny a reward that has been agreed and earned.

- Your child will appreciate that taking care of their teeth can be fun, and these positive early habits will help to encourage good dental health and routine throughout their lives.

## About the Author

Dr Sarah Kasasa is a dental surgeon in clinical practice in London. She has a PhD from King's College London and is a peer-reviewed research author with over 20 years' experience working in oral health. One of her main passions is education around childhood dental health, and she has special expertise on the impact of nutrition and lifestyle on disease prevention.

ISBN 978-1-78270-210-8

Copyright © Award Publications Limited

All rights reserved. No part of this publication may be reproduced or utilised in any form or by any means electronic or mechanical, including photocopying, recording, or by any information storage and retrieval system now known or hereafter invented, without the prior written permission of the publisher.

Published by Award Publications Limited,
The Old Riding School, Welbeck,
Worksop, S80 3LR

/awardpublications   @award.books   @award_books
www.awardpublications.co.uk

23-1072 4

Printed in China

# The Children's Book of
# DENTAL HEALTH

Dr Sarah Kasasa, PhD

Illustrated by Helen Stanton

award

# Healthy Teeth

Teeth are very important. They help us to chew our food and to speak properly. We need to make sure that we keep them clean by brushing them twice a day. This also helps keep our gums healthy, our breath fresh, and our smiles looking great!

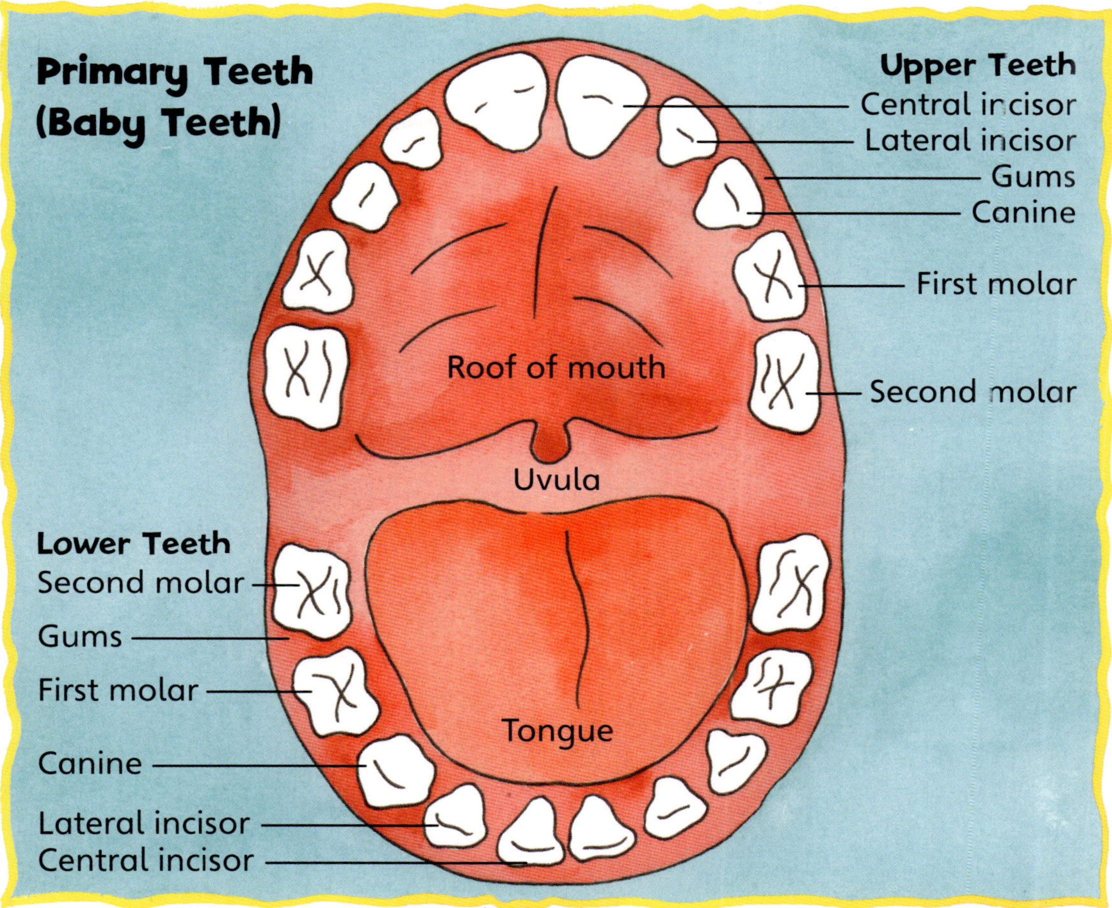

# Your Teeth

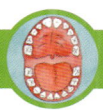

**Primary Teeth (Baby Teeth)**

**Upper Teeth**
- Central incisor
- Lateral incisor
- Gums
- Canine
- First molar
- Second molar

Roof of mouth

Uvula

**Lower Teeth**
- Second molar
- Gums
- First molar
- Canine
- Lateral incisor
- Central incisor

Tongue

At around 6 months old, our 'baby teeth' start to come through. There are usually 20, in different shapes and sizes – incisors are sharp and straight for biting, while molars are wider and flatter for chewing. From age 6, baby teeth start to fall out and permanent teeth appear. No more grow after that, so we have to look after them!

**Not Brushing Teeth in the Morning**

Jack eats sugary breakfast cereal and doesn't leave enough time to brush his teeth before school. His classmates won't sit next to him and this makes him sad. His friend Ali explains politely that his breath smells. **Why does Jack's breath smell bad?**

# Making Time to Brush Your Teeth

Jack's mum makes him porridge for breakfast and he makes sure to leave plenty of time to brush his teeth after eating. His breath smells fresh and he has lots of fun joining in with his friends. **Do you brush your teeth every morning?**

I make time to brush my teeth

# Not Brushing Teeth Properly

Leah always remembers to brush her teeth in the morning and before bed, and so she cannot understand why some of her teeth are yellow. Her dad realises that Leah is not brushing her teeth correctly and plaque is building up on her teeth.
**Why are Leah's teeth yellow?**

# Using the Right Technique

Leah's dad shows her how to brush her teeth in a circular motion and gives her a timer to make sure that she brushes for at least two minutes. Leah's teeth start to look whiter and are much healthier.

**Why is it important to brush your teeth thoroughly?**

I brush for two minutes

**Not Visiting the Dentist**

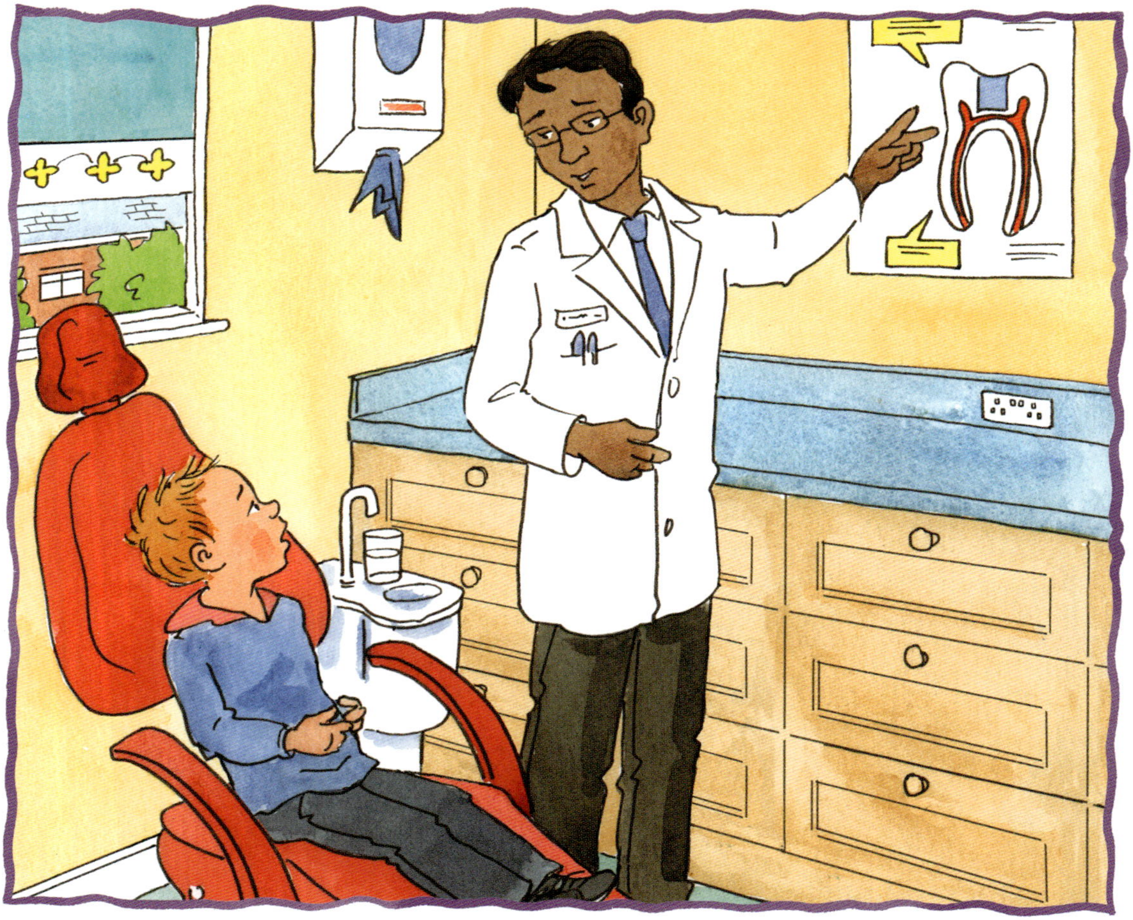

Luca thinks he only has to see a dentist when his teeth hurt. When he does go, his dentist tells him he has a cavity and needs a filling. The tooth is fixed, but Luca is sad that he needed to have a filling. **Why should you visit the dentist for regular check-ups?**

# Visiting the Dentist Regularly

Luca's friend Tom tells him that he goes to the dentist for a check-up every six months, as this helps keep his teeth healthy. He knows his dentist well and gets a sticker each time he goes.

**How often should you visit your dentist?**

## Eating Too Many Sugary Foods

Emily's family often visit the cinema and always have lots of treats, such as chocolate and ice cream. But sweeter and fast foods often contain lots of sugar, which can lead to cavities, and weight gain too. **Why shouldn't you eat too many unhealthy foods?**

# Finding the Right Balance

Emily and Noah try to eat more healthy foods when they go to the cinema. They have dried fruit and sometimes their parents buy them some chocolate as a treat. They know they can have treats as long as it is not too often.

**Do you have a balanced diet?**

I cut down on sugary snacks

# Sucking Thumbs

Chloe sucks her thumb at night and when she is upset. Her sister Zoe notices that her teeth are starting to point forwards. Zoe's teeth are crooked too because she didn't give up her dummy until she was three years old. **Why are Chloe's teeth moving out of place?**

# Breaking Bad Habits

Chloe's mum buys her a cute soft toy to cuddle, and gives her a sticker for every day she manages not to suck her thumb. Slowly, Chloe grows out of the habit and her teeth straighten naturally.

**How can bad habits affect our teeth?**

# Having Sugary Drinks

Arash loves fizzy drinks and has them every day. He often needs fillings in his teeth. When he visits his dentist she tells him that the sugar and acid in the drinks are making his teeth decay quickly and develop cavities.

**Why does he need fillings?**

# Drinking Healthy Drinks

Arash tries the dentist's suggestions and switches to water and milk instead of fizzy drinks. His mouth is healthier and at his next check-up he doesn't need any more treatment.

**What is your favourite healthy drink?**

I drink healthy drinks

# Not Brushing Babies' Teeth

Lily's aunt and uncle visit for the weekend with their twins. The babies drink milk and juice from bottles and their parents don't brush their teeth at bedtime. The twins have toothache and cry at night, keeping Lily and her family awake.

**Why are the twins in pain?**

# Brushing Babies' Teeth

After talking to their dentist, Lily's aunt and uncle give the twins baby cups to drink from instead of bottles. They always brush the babies' teeth too. The twins are happy babies and their teeth and gums are healthy.

**Do you drink from a cup?**

I drink from a cup

# Not Getting Enough Calcium

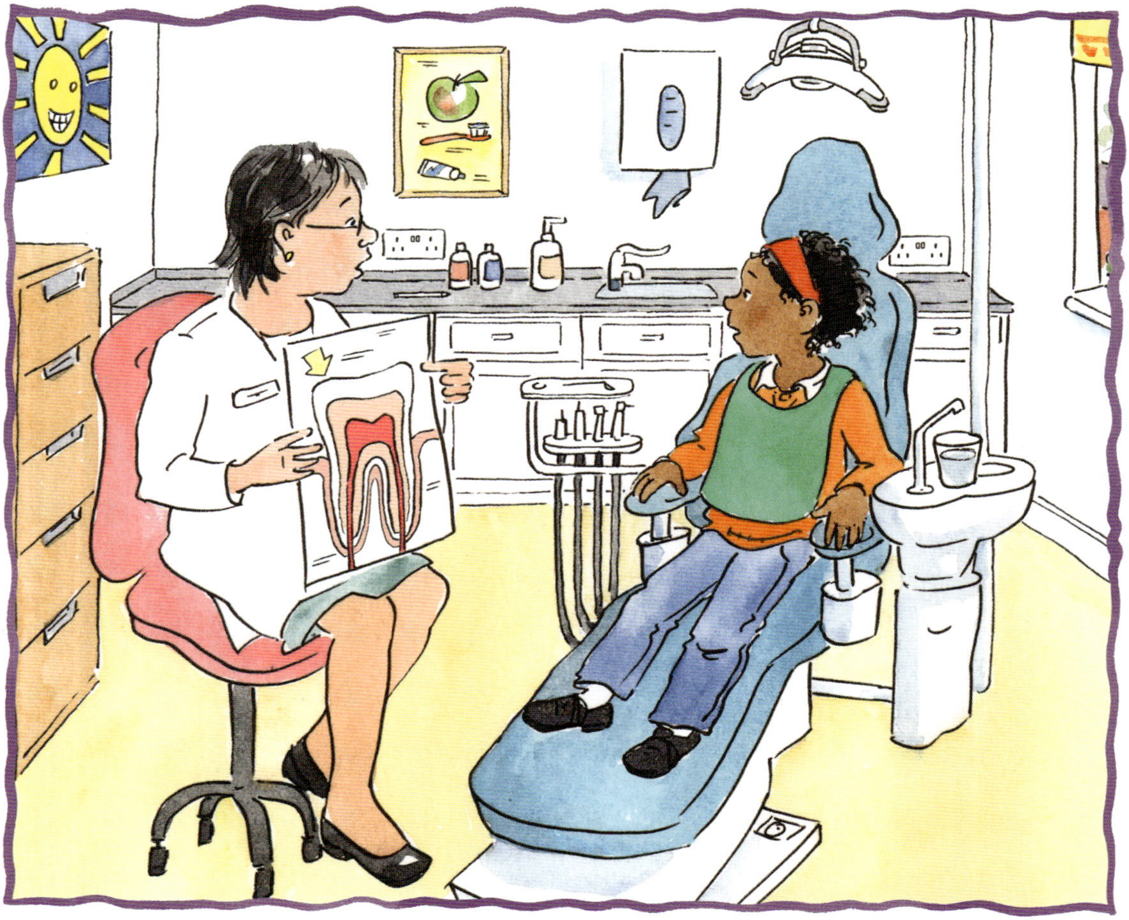

Lisa's dentist tells her at her check-up that the enamel on her teeth is not very strong and there is a high risk she will develop lots of cavities. She tells Lisa it's probably because she is not getting enough calcium. **Why is it important to eat calcium-rich foods?**

# Keeping Teeth Strong and Healthy

Lisa tries to have plenty of calcium-rich foods, such as milk, cheese, yogurt, oranges, almonds and green vegetables. At her next check-up, Lisa's dentist is pleased that her teeth are looking stronger and healthier.
**Do you get lots of calcium?**

## Eating Soft and Processed Foods

Abdul prefers soft foods, and loves ready meals and takeaways. But they're not hard or crunchy enough to help his baby teeth fall out. Mum notices that his baby teeth are crowding his new adult teeth.

**Why isn't Abdul losing his baby teeth?**

**Losing Baby Teeth**

Abdul's mum checks with the dentist, who says he needs to eat foods with different textures. Abdul tries some firmer, crunchier foods, such as celery and carrot sticks. His baby teeth slowly start to fall out naturally.
**Do you eat foods with different textures?**

I eat a variety of foods

# Not Flossing Your Teeth

The dentist tells Farida's mum that she has a problem with a build-up of plaque and food around her teeth. Farida tells her mum that the dental floss at home is too fiddly and she is not sure how to use it correctly. **Why should you floss your teeth?**

# Flossing Your Teeth

Farida's mum buys flossers with handles, which are easier to use. She helps Farida floss her teeth at least once a day, until she is able to do it by herself.
Farida's teeth become cleaner and much healthier.

**How often should you floss?**

## Not Having Braces

Kai's dentist tells him he needs braces to help straighten his teeth, but Kai is worried and doesn't want them. When his aunt comes over, he sees her teeth are crooked. She says she never had braces as a child. **Why do some people need braces?**

# Straight Teeth

Kai has braces fitted. He has to take extra care cleaning his teeth, but he soon gets used to them. When the braces come off, his teeth are straight. He feels confident and happy with his nice smile.

**Do you follow your dentist's advice?**

# Losing a Tooth During Sport

Mo's sister Ava loves to play hockey, but she has forgotten to bring her mouthguard to the game. She plays anyway and a player accidentally knocks into her. Her mouth is bleeding and a tooth has fallen out.
**Why should you wear protective sports equipment?**

# Wearing Protective Equipment

Ava takes the time before the game to make sure that she has packed her mouthguard with her sports kit. She promises her mum that she will not play if she ever forgets to take it to a game.
**Can you think of any sports for which you need a mouthguard?**

I protect my teeth

## Too Tired or Busy to Brush at Bedtime

Ethan and his sister Kim are often too tired or too busy playing to brush their teeth at bedtime. The bacteria left in their mouths overnight cause damage to their teeth and gums. When they do remember to brush, their gums bleed.
**Why do their gums bleed?**

# Making Time to Brush at Bedtime

Ethan and Kim's mum makes sure they always stop playing five minutes before bedtime to brush their teeth. Brushing properly with toothpaste gets rid of bacteria, and their gums no longer bleed. **Do you brush your teeth every evening?**

I brush my teeth before bed

# Glossary

**Acid damage** – when acid in foods and drinks begins to dissolve tooth enamel.

**Bacteria** – tiny organisms that live in our mouths.

**Braces** – a specially made device that is attached to teeth to help straighten or move them.

**Calcium** – a mineral that makes teeth hard and strong.

**Cavities** – holes in teeth.

**Decay** – damage to teeth caused by bacteria.

**Enamel** – the hard outer surface of a tooth.

**Filling** – a white or silver material that is used to fill a hole in a tooth.

**Gums** – the flesh around the teeth.

**Mouthguard** – a plastic shield that covers teeth to protect them. The ones used to protect from sports injuries are often called sports mouthguards.

**Plaque** – a sticky, cream-coloured film that forms on teeth. Plaque is made up of food and bacteria.

**Toothache** – pain as a result of tooth decay, or from an infection in a tooth or gums.

**Toothbrush** – a long-handled brush with bristles at one end, used with toothpaste to clean teeth and gums.

**Toothpaste** – the soft gel or paste used to clean teeth and freshen breath.

Encourage your child to use the picture stickers and answer the questions in the book.

I floss every day

I visit the dentist regularly

I brush for two minutes

I drink from a cup

I drink healthy drinks

I cut down on sugary snacks

I get enough calcium

I break bad habits

I am brave when having treatment

I make time to brush my teeth

I protect my teeth

I eat a variety of foods

I brush my teeth before bed

Use these gold star stickers to praise your child's efforts and encourage their progress.